THE HOVERCRAFT

PHOTOGRAPHS FROM THE ARCHIVES OF THE WORLD'S ONLY HOVERCRAFT MUSEUM

JIM GRAY

AMBERLEY

First published 2017

Amberley Publishing
The Hill, Stroud
Gloucestershire, GL5 4EP

www.amberley-books.com

Copyright © Jim Gray, 2017

The right of Jim Gray to be identified as
the Author of this work has been asserted in
accordance with the Copyrights, Designs and
Patents Act 1988.

ISBN 978 1 4456 7276 2 (print)
ISBN 978 1 4456 7277 9 (ebook)

British Library Cataloguing in Publication Data.
A catalogue record for this book is available from
the British Library.

Origination by Amberley Publishing.
Printed in the UK.

Contents

Foreword

The book has been printed to raise money for the further development of the UK's only hovercraft museum. The museum is a charity and receives no grants; its sole income is from visits, donations and the sale of goods.

It is managed entirely by volunteers, and this book is dedicated to them for selflessly giving their time and skills to ensure that the museum develops and runs smoothly. We have volunteers who are responsible for the engineering, restoration, and maintenance of craft; those who manage the shop; those who maintain the site and grounds; those who give tours and are always around to give information on craft when required. They all try to enhance visits and provide quality customer care. Finally we have a board of unpaid trustees who work tirelessly to ensure the museum continues to evolve. They give a clear sense of direction and do their best to support the work of all volunteers.

The photographs have come from the archives of the museum and as such they belong to the nation. They have been taken by a number of photographers over the last sixty years and form the first volume of 'Photographs from the Archives.' There are some iconic images that fire the imagination and bring the past to life. They also serve to heighten our appreciation of the significance of the craft that have been saved and are now on display at the museum.

This book has been written and compiled by Jim Gray with the support and encouragement of trustees and friends of the museum. I would like to thank John Harnett for proofreading and for his help in locating photographs and Stewart England for his meticulous work and advice in the editing of them. I am indebted to Warwick Jacobs for always trying to answer the awkward question and a special word of thanks must go to Steve Henderson. Steve, a trustee, not only proofread the book but has also been a solid pillar of support throughout; always available and helpful. Finally, but not least, thanks to my wife Tricia for her understanding and encouragement.

Introduction

Along the seafront of Lee-on-the-Solent, opposite the slipway, lies an entrance to what was HMS *Daedalus* but what now leads to the Hovercraft Museum – the only hovercraft museum in the UK and, indeed, the world. It is fitting that it is situated on the very site of HMS *Daedalus*, where hovercraft were evaluated and maintained. Lee-on-the-Solent is synonymous with planes and in particular sea planes. It is also very much the home of the hovercraft.

After the first cross-channel crossing by a hovercraft in 1959 there was a revolution in hovercraft design and development, both commercial and military. Within ten years we had the mighty SRN4, which crossed the channel regularly in under forty minutes and which could carry over 400 passengers and sixty cars. Military hovercraft had developed and there was an Army hovercraft squadron formed, 200 Hovercraft Squadron RCT, based along the road at Browndown. Small as well as large craft appeared as many hovercraft manufacturers and developers appeared along the Solent. The world-renowned Mackace hoverplatform was based at Funtley; the Pindair Skima range was based at Gosport; the mighty Saunders Roe and later BHC at Cowes – to name but a few of the many scattered along the Solent.

As hovercraft developed after 1959 at an unbelievable pace, right at the centre was Lee-on-the-Solent. In 1961 the British Interservice Hovercraft (Trials) Unit (IHTU) had been established on HMS *Daedalus* (known as HMS *Ariel* from 1959 to 1965) with personnel drawn from the Army, Royal Marines, Royal Navy and the RAF. From 1968 it became known as the IHU. Extensive use was made of the widened and improved slipway as hovercraft came and went. The purpose of the Unit was to enable service personnel to gain experience of hovercraft and to assist manufacturers in development while evaluating any military potential of the hovercraft. Hence a wide range of craft, commercial and military, passed up and down that slipway and would be seen showing their paces in the Solent.

The hovercraft was quite different from any other form of transport that had been seen before – perhaps that is one reason it seemed to grab the imagination of the public and draw crowds wherever it appeared. The man responsible for this revolutionary craft was Sir Christopher Cockerell, who demonstrated that a cushion of air could be generated and maintained under a moving object so that it was completely free of surface drag. In 1956 he demonstrated his first working model and only three years later, on 25 July 1959, the world's first hovercraft, the SRN1, crossed the English Channel. The hovercraft had arrived!

Revolutions tend not to last long and such was the case with the hovercraft. By 2000 the last of the cross-channel ferries had gone, but the first scheduled hovercraft service, which has run from the mainland to the Isle of Wight since 1965, continues to operate. Griffon Hovercraft continue to be built on the Solent and both military and commercial hovercraft are still used, though mainly abroad. Recreational and small hovercraft remain very popular.

The museum at Lee-on-the-Solent has more than seventy historic craft on display and also houses extensive archives revealing the story behind the hovercraft. These photographs from the archives hopefully tell the story of the excitement, the history, the importance and the impact hovercraft have had and the fascination held by the public to this very day, in a way that words never could. It should also remind us of the importance of Lee-on-the-Solent in hovercraft history.

Memorable Arrivals and Departures from the Slipway at Lee-on-the-Solent

March, 1962. A naval rating signals 'Halt' to more conventional traffic as the Saunders-Roe SRN1 crosses the main seafront road at Lee-on-the-Solent and returns to HMS *Ariel* (later reverted to HMS *Daedalus* in 1965, and now the site of the Hovercraft Museum). She had started trials with the Interservice Hovercraft Trials Unit and roles such as anti-submarine warfare, air-sea rescue and mine counter measures were foreseen.

SRN3 comes up the slipway after trials in the Solent and returns to the Interservice Hovercraft Trials Unit at HMS *Daedalus*.

SRN5 leaves HMS *Daedalus*, crossing the seafront road and, like so many seaplanes and earlier hovercraft, going down the slipway into the Solent for further trials.

2004. *Beasac III*, the SRN6 Mk6 or 'The Twin Prop', comes up the slipway to her new home at the museum, where she can still be admired today, after a journey from Belgium. It was the fastest SRN6 built and the last gas turbine hovercraft to cross the channel.

June, 1994. The SRN4 Mk2 Swift is pulled up the slipway to her final resting place at the museum. Sadly she was broken up in 2004.

1989. BH7 Mk2, built in 1967 at Woolston and launched in 1969, comes up the slipway at Lee-on-the-Solent for the final time. She still looks out to sea from her current site at the museum and visitors can board and admire a craft fitted with operational mine hunting kit and that flew to the Arctic Circle and back from Lee in 1972.

Historic Groups of Hovercraft

Right: 1982. An SRN6, a BH7 and a VT2 (Vosper Thorneycroft 2) speed along the Solent. A magnificent sight! It is also an historic photograph as the three craft travelled in close formation along the Solent and past Daedalus Slipway at Lee-on-the-Solent at the closing of the Naval Hovercraft Trials Unit based at HMS *Daedalus*.

Below: Two Naval hovercraft – an SRN6 Mk2 hovercraft with soft-top and a BH7 – go through their paces in the Solent.

The SRN6 Mk6, the Twin Prop now in the museum, the VT2 and the BH7.

Five historic hovercraft: SRN5s on the outside and SRN6s on the inside, with the SRN3 in the centre.

Hovershow, 1966. The SRN3, SRN6 and SRN5 speed along the Stokes Bay coastline and show how quickly hovercraft have developed since 1959.

Two SRN6s are followed by two SRN5s along the Solent.

1966. An SRN1, SRN2 and SRN3 compete for star of the Hovershow.

1966. From left to right: SRN5, SRN6, SRN3, CC4, SRN5, SRN6, HD1 and CC2.
    The HD1 was the first non-amphibious sidewall craft. It was a 9-ton development craft built at Hythe to test skirts and flexible side bodies.

From left to right: an SRN2, SRN5 and SRN1. HMS *Daedalus* held a 'mini Farnborough' in 1964 when this photograph was taken.

The SRN5 sitting at *Daedalus* alongside the SRN3. They were both being tested by the Interservice Hovercraft Trials Unit.

The HD2 in the centre was a full-size test vehicle to research and test hovercraft controls. It was built in 1966 and is currently being restored at the museum. It is flanked by two Cushioncraft: the CC4 and the larger CC7. The photograph was taken at an open day held by HDL (Hovercraft Development Ltd) based at Hythe, where the HD1 and HD2 were developed.

A photograph taken on the slipway of BHC (British Hovercraft Corporation) on the Isle of Wight. It shows three SRN6 craft: one belonging to Hovertravel (026), a BHC craft (016) and a craft (018) from Aeronave (Naples).

This was taken in January 1964 and shows the SRN3 and a Denny D2 at Westland's slipway, Cowes.

1974. Sioux helicopters of the Blue Eagles display team fly over the sea cadet training ship *Royalist*, and a military SRN6 hovercraft. It was a flypast to mark the demise of 200 Hovercraft Trials Squadron RCT based at Browndown, Gosport.

Hovercraft on the River Thames

May 1960: SRN1, the first hovercraft, on the Thames during the Commonwealth Prime Ministers' Conference.

The sight of SRN1 on the Thames signalled the rapid development of hovercraft.

Denny D2 'Hoverbus', built on the Clyde, passes the Houses of Parliament and shows one of the many uses of the hovercraft. She travelled all the way from the Clyde down to the Thames under her own power.

Hoverlloyd's SRN4 *Sure* on a visit to London in October 1970. *Sure* was built in 1969 and converted to a Mk2 in 1974 before being broken up in 1983.

This time it is the turn of the SRN4 *The Princess Margaret* to turn heads on the Thames. She was built in 1968 and was 'stretched' and relaunched as a Mk3 in 1978. She was in service until 2000 when she came to the museum. Sadly, she is likely to be broken up in 2017.

SRN1

Sir Christopher Cockerell, the inventor of the hovercraft, seen in 1956 with a model being tested on the Pergola lawn at Somerleyton Hall. Here he had the privacy to gather information and to give working demonstrations. Eventually a contract was placed with Saunders-Roe to evaluate the concept and later to build a larger experimental craft – the SRN1.

1959. Sir Christopher Cockerell at the front of the SRN1 without a skirt. Note the height of the hover.

He was to be knighted in 1966 and was granted fifty-nine patents for Hovercraft inventions alone, as well as three for Wavepower services. During the SRN1's progressive development, five distinct versions evolved, each bringing significant technical advances over its predecessor. Originally designed to operate at 25 knots at a weight of 4 tons, the final version was operating at almost twice the weight and over twice the speed.

The SRN1 on display at Farnborough in 1959 alongside the sole prototype Fairey Rotodyne, which featured a tip jet-powered rotor.

July 25, 1959. The SRN1 can be seen approaching Calais before making its historic crossing to Dover. The date was the fiftieth anniversary of Louis Blériot's cross-channel flight. As well as the test pilot and navigator, Cockerell provided inventive ballast by carefully positioning himself as required.

July 25, 1959. An interested crowd at Calais inspect Britain's 'flying saucer' as it waits for favourable weather to make the first crossing of the English Channel under its own power. It was to cross the water to Dover – twenty-one miles – in two hours and three minutes. The flight proved the craft's capabilities but also its initial limitations. It wasn't until 1961 when the flexible skirt was invented that air cushion technology really took off.

February, 1963. This SRN1 Mk5 with its 5-foot skirt can be seen in Osborne Bay, Isle of Wight, near Queen Victoria's former residence.

SRN2

The SRN2 next to a Sycamore helicopter in February 1963. It first flew in 1961. It weighed 27 tons and could carry forty-eight passengers. It can be regarded as the prototype for future commercial hovercraft.

13 August, 1962. Passengers disembarking on the first run of the new Hovercraft Service between Appley Tower, Ryde, Isle of Wight, and Eastney beach, Southsea. It made the journey in fifteen minutes. In 1964 it also ran when a new service from Eastney to Ryde operated under Hovertransport.

18 August, 1962. SRN2 coming ashore at Appley beach, Ryde. In August 1962 Westland Aircraft and Southdown Motor Services operated this experimental service between Eastney beach, Southsea, and Appley beach, Ryde. SRN2 was used for two hours a day for eight days, carrying 1,554 passengers. Hovercraft captured the imagination of the public, as can be seen in the interest shown.

21 July, 1964. The SRN2 near the mouth of the Beaulieu River. Roles envisaged for the craft included passenger ferry, freight carrier, survey work and offshore supply services.

January, 1963. The SRN2 can be seen operating over pack ice in Wooton Creek, Isle of Wight. Icing tests at sub-zero water and air temperatures, following the coldest night for more than sixty years, showed that the craft's operation at normal speeds and hovering heights was not impaired.

Above: 1963. A passenger service was being trialled between Weston-super-Mare and Penarth, five miles west of Cardiff, and here is the SRN2 landing at Penarth.

Left: May, 1962. The SRN2 off loading at Victoria Pier, Montreal, Canada.

1962. The SRN2 in Canada showing her capabilities demonstrating on the Lachine Rapids on the St Lawrence River. Here it made history with the first high-speed crossing of the rapids, travelling at over 40 knots.

SRN3

November, 1963. SRN3 hovercraft. This 37½ ton craft was fitted with 4-foot skirts and, at the time, was the largest hovercraft in the world. It was the sole prototype, built specifically for military applications and used for evaluation purposes by the Interservice Hovercraft Trials Unit. It was envisaged for uses such as a military patrol boat, or as a high-speed and amphibious military load-carrying craft.

January, 1964. Here you can see three generations of craft. In the foreground is the SRN1, in the middle the SRN2 and beyond is the SRN3. The SRN3 was over 23 metres in length, the SRN2 over 19 metres, and the SRN1 measured 12.5 metres.

June, 1966. The SRN3 can be seen alongside a CC4 craft at the Hovershow Exhibition at Browndown, Stokes Bay, in 1966. The Hovershow held in June 1966 was the world's first hovershow and was intended to promote export sales of hovercraft. In seven years hovercraft had developed at a pace no one could have imagined. The show was opened by Lord Mountbatten and was open five days, the last two to the general public.

The SRN3 executed 570 sorties in the course of her trials history between 1964 and her final sortie in February 1974. She covered an estimated 40,000 nautical miles in Danish, German and UK waters and laid the foundation from which subsequent craft were developed. In one of her early trials she carried two long-wheelbase Land Rovers and fifty-four passengers at an average speed of 54 knots.

1974. The final trial! Look carefully and you will see that the SRN3 is tethered before being subjected to a series of large mine explosions. The relative invulnerability of hovercraft to underwater explosions was about to be tested. Two of the main engines, all portable equipment and any other equipment useful to other craft were removed. She was not expected to return!

The mines exploded but the SRN3 proved she was virtually unsinkable and did indeed return to base. Indeed the last half-a-mile-or-so onto the slipway was under her own power. Sadly it was in vain and the one and only SRN3 was broken up at HMS *Daedalus*.

SRN5

The SRN5 (or Warden class) first flew in 1964. It was the first production-built hovercraft in the world. The one above, 006, was used by the Interservice Hovercraft Trials Unit. It is the only one left in the UK. It was acquired by the museum in 1986 and has been caringly restored. This craft was used to demonstrate the SRN5 worldwide and more than fifty pilots were trained in her.

It was this cutting-edge craft that spread the use of hovercraft around the world – mainly for military and coastguard use. Fourteen SRN5s were produced, of which four entered service with the Interservice Hovercraft Trials Unit. The fifteen-seater was to pave the way for future developments, with the basic design stretched to become the thirty-eight-seat SRN6, named the Winchester class.

This SRN5 (XV657) was one of the four that entered service with the Interservice Hovercraft Trials Unit. She first put to sea in October 1964 and was delivered to the Interservice Hovercraft Trials Unit in March, 1965. This craft had a double association with royalty. In 1965 at the Amsterdam Trade Fair, Queen Juliana, Prince Bernhardt and Princess Margaret went for a ride on the craft. Then in July, 1965 she was used to transport Her Majesty Queen Elizabeth II from Yarmouth on the Isle of Wight to RAF Thorney Island, near Chichester. She is shown here carrying out a rescue drill.

1966. This photograph was taken at Tuktoyaktuk. The Canadian Coast Guard used an SRN5 for rescue and survey work for twenty years. Tuktoyaktuk is situated north of the Arctic Circle, on the shore of the Beaufort Sea.

1966. Canadian trials with the SRN5, prior to the purchase of one.

An SRN5 on exercise at Browndown with 200 Hovercraft Squadron RCT.

1975. The museum SRN5 craft (006). The year is 1975 and she is operating as a tender in the Wash, where there was civil construction work. Note the split barge.

SRN6

The SRN6 was the first production craft to enter commercial service. It was the most produced and proved to be a real workhorse. It was compact, highly manoeuvrable and fully amphibious. It was modified and used in a variety of roles, both military and commercial. This photograph, taken in 1968, shows the prototype SRN6 three years after its launch in March 1965. It was basically a stretched SRN5, offering more seating capacity and greater load space. They operated passenger routes both across the channel and from Portsmouth to the Isle of Wight. This prototype is on display at the museum.

This is a photograph of an SRN6 Mk6. It is known as 'The Twin Prop' or 'Super 6'. This was the fastest SRN6 built. This version had twin propellers, and its length was increased and sides modified. It was a quieter hovercraft than its single-prop sisters.

This SRN6 (018) made the journey from Dakar to the Ivory Coast by rivers and land in 1970. The expedition was led by David Smithers and flown by Captain Peter Ayles. The Trans-African expedition was to take them through eight West African countries and was to be the longest and most ambitious hovercraft journey ever. From October 1969 to January 1970 they covered 5,000 miles, opening up a waterway never seen before. The craft survived the expedition only to be wrecked by a large wave on press day. The British Army took over the hovercraft at the end of the expedition and shipped it to the Ivory Coast for trials in heavy surf. It was wrecked as she came ashore at Abidjan.

An SRN6 attracts attention at Expo 67 at Montreal. Two SR-N6s were provided by Hoverwork to ferry visitors around the site on the St Lawrence River. The craft operated for the full six months of the world's largest fair, working thirteen hours a day, seven days a week. They were providing the 3½ mile service using three terminals around the site on the St Lawrence River.

SRN6 009. Another view of the prototype SRN6 Mk1 in 1965, which is on display in the museum. In the photograph it can be seen at Columbine Slipway, east Cowes. The craft has a fascinating history, operating in Norway, from Cowes to Southampton and also on the Portsmouth-to-the-Island route. It was also the first craft stretched to become the SRN6 Mk1S. This photograph was clearly taken shortly after her launch in 1965 as there are no puffports to be seen. Note the SRN1 hovercraft in the background.

An SRN6 (014) completed in 1965 and leased to Shell, operating in Brunei doing offshore oil rig work. The craft was then sold in 1969 to the New Zealand government and extensively modified for rescue work and worked for a while at Auckland Airport. There was a real need for a hovercraft as the airport was built next to Manakau Harbour, which surrounds the airport on three sides – hence the problem of mudflats and tidal waters. Indeed, in 1966 the first hovercraft to visit New Zealand (the museum's SRN5) had rescued a parachutist from Manakau Harbour.

Above: February, 1968. This is an
SRN6 Mk2 carrying out surf trials at
Saunton Sands on the North Devon
coast.

Right: The prototype SRN6 (009)
was operated by Scandinavian
Hovercraft Promotions under the
name 'Scanhover'. It entered service in
1965 and was later joined by a second
craft. They operated on a 120-mile
route, with six stopping points, in the
Alesund area.

In February, 1966 a six-week Cold Weather Trials was carried out by Scanhover with SRN6 Mk1 009. The first three weeks were spent at Malmö and the remainder of the tour north of Stockholm and in the Stockholm archipelago. Typical performances recorded were: speeds of over 70 knots over smooth ice, and speeds of up to 25 knots over ridges of ice up to 1.07 m in height. In addition the craft operated successfully over loose snow up to 0.9 m. Note there is only one set of puffports at the stern. They were added to the bow later.

This SRN6 is loaded onto a road trailer en route to Scotland. The hovercraft is carried on Bedford lorries, the skirt requiring a lorry of its own.

This SRN6 is en route to Abu Dhabi. The year is 1977.

This ambulance livery was for demonstration purposes but reflects the potential of the SRN6 to fulfil a wide range of roles.

Hovercraft at Shatt Al-Arab, Abadan, Iran, 1970. Eight SRN6s had been sold to the Imperial Iranian Navy (numbers 040 to 047). Here they can be seen in impressive formation, armed and on exercise. They were used effectively in a wide range of roles including search and rescue, interception, flood relief and logistics support along the Iranian coastline.

SRN4

The SRN4, or Mountbatten class, first commenced trials in February 1968 and by June had made its first crossing to France. Within ten years it showed how rapidly hovercraft had developed since the SRN1. The SRN4 symbolised the hopes and aspirations of the entire industry and it was not to disappoint. In the photograph are *Swift* and *Sure*. The cost of a crossing in 1978 was £7.80 for an adult day return or £19 for a car with driver and up to four passengers for a single crossing.

The SRN4s were called Mountbatten class in recognition of the contribution Lord Mountbatten made to the hovercraft industry. From the early days of development, when he was First Sea Lord, he saw the potential and actively encouraged its development. The SRN4s were to run for over thirty years and the six built carried over 80 million passengers and 18 million vehicles.

The Princess Anne was built at Cowes by BHC (British Hovercraft Corporation) and was named by Princess Anne in October 1969. In 1977/8 she was stretched and refitted, increasing the number of passengers from 250 to 418 and the number of cars from thirty to sixty.

In September, 1995, *The Princess Anne* took the 'official' world record for the fastest channel crossing, completing the journey in twenty-two minutes. The speed limit was 70 mph and there is little doubt there were faster crossings, with *Swift* reputed to have done it in just over fifteen minutes. The regular crossing time was thirty-five to forty minutes!

The Princess Margaret, an SRN4 Mk 3 (stretched), sits alongside N500. The N500 was a French craft built for the cross-channel route. Only two were built and one was destroyed by fire before entering service. Sadly the other proved unreliable and was broken up in 1985.

In total there were six SRN4s, but only two Mk3s (stretched) owned by Seaspeed; the other four, which ended their lives as MK2s, were owned by Hoverlloyd. They were built by BHC at Cowes. The first SRN4 in service, *The Princess Margaret*, operated from 1968 to 2000 – when she came to the Hovercraft Museum.

The Princess Anne's propellers measure 21 feet and are the largest in the world. She operated from 1969 to October 2000. In December 2000 she came to the Hovercraft Museum, where she can still be appreciated by visitors.

The Princess Anne was the fourth SRN4 built at BHC Cowes. The other five were: *The Princess Margaret, Swift, Sure, The Sir Christopher* and *The Prince of Wales*.

The 'stretching' of *The Princess Anne* in 1977/8. A middle section was added, increasing its length by 55 feet to 185 feet (39.6 metres). The cost of the stretch was said to be £12 million. In the foreground the section being built for the stretching of *The Princess Margaret* can be seen.

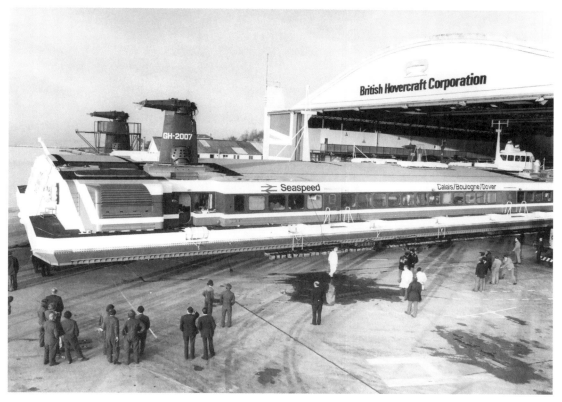

GH 2007 (*The Princess Anne*) emerges minus her skirt after the stretch. Her skirts would weigh 30 tons!

BH7

1989. BH7 Mk2 (XW255 P235), 23.9 m long and 13.9 m wide, returns, with some help, to *Daedalus* for the final time. She can be seen here having her skirt inflated. Both the BH7 and the green blower can still be seen by visitors at the museum.

This is the craft that can now be seen at the museum. It was designed solely for military operations and was trialled in various roles from 1970 to 1983, operating in fast attack, patrol work, mine countermeasures, anti-submarine warfare and fishery protection. It was also fitted with a microwave – the first microwave on any warship! It is still in the galley today. It is the sole prototype of the BH7 class.

BH7 Mk5A – a craft destined for the Iranian Navy. She is seen during tests prior to being shipped to Iran. The BH7 incorporates many of the components and systems used in the SRN4, and in design concept could almost be described in effect as a quarter-size version of the SRN4. It had the same 21-foot propeller and the gas turbine engine. This speed and secure design with the military adaptions made it a reliable and more than useful craft.

1974. GH 9003, a Mk5A, one of the six BH7s built for the navy of Iran. Two of the six were seen in exercises as late as 2002. The coastal patrol craft was fast, could be armed with missiles and offered versatility. It was capable of transporting sixty troops and equipment.

The same hovercraft, this time demonstrating how the wide side decks can accommodate a variety of medium-range surface-to-surface missiles.

The BH7 flies past the *Royalist*, a sail training ship launched in 1971 and replaced in 2014.

This photograph speaks louder than words. The BH7, the SRN6 and the Wessex helicopter pass the Needles. A wonderful sight!

The Welldeck, SRN6 Mk5

The SRN6 Mk5, better known as a 'Welldeck' craft. In order to overcome shortcomings in a vehicle carrier in logistic support and amphibious roles, financial constraints led to the conversion of SR-N5s in 1971/2 to create the Welldeck. Two 'new' craft resulted – XT657 and XT493. The resulting craft were some 5 feet longer. XT493 has survived and can be seen at the museum. The photograph shows the craft XT657 on exercise in Norway in 1973.

During exercises, as well as being used to carry vehicles and support weapons it was also used to move troops. As many as fifty-five troops were carried in the Welldeck.

On exercise with 200 Squadron RCT in 1973. During the exercise the craft covered some 2,670 nautical miles and carried 765 passengers and 107 tons of cargo. This exercise was 150 miles inside the Arctic Circle, but thankfully in a generally mild winter!

A close-up of the Welldeck. Its length is 16.1 m, with a maximum speed of 50 knots.

AP1-88

The AP1-88 was the craft that replaced the SRN6 on the Southsea-to-Ryde route and is well known in the Solent. The Southsea-to-Ryde service is the only scheduled hovercraft passenger service in Europe and is operated by Hovertravel, the world's longest running commercial hovercraft service. The AP1-88 was itself replaced in 2016 by the Griffon 1200TD.

The AP1-88 in 2016, alongside the Griffon 1200TD craft about to replace it. The AP1-88 replaced the workhorse SRN6 and provided a quieter and more efficient craft with greater seating capacity. It seated up to 101 passengers and was 21.5 m in length, powered by two air-cooled turbo-diesel engines. It has also run a service from Sweden to Denmark.

AP1- 88/200 (GH 9033) *Waban-Aki*. This craft was bought in 1996 for the Canadian Castguard. It was based at Quebec and in 2010 was sold to Griffon Hoverwork, then sold on to a company in Venezuela, and renamed with the intention of operating on the River Orinoco. However, she was not used in Venezuela. The photograph shows her at Cowes.

VA Hovercraft

1961. An experimental hovercraft built by Vickers-Armstrong, the VA-1 is seen here undergoing tests. This was one of several Air Cushioned Vehicles (ACVs) chartered by the Interservice Hovercraft Trials Unit for familiarisation and evaluation. The craft was unsophisticated but proved important to Vickers-Armstrong in research terms for future developments.

The VA-1 first left the ground in 1960 at a loaded weight of 1500 kg and with a hovering height of 11.5 cm. From little acorns... it was 7.62 m long and 3.96 m wide, with a cruising speed of 45 mph. It was the first rectangular hovercraft and was constructed mainly from resin-bonded plywood. It was intended as a research platform. She is seen here at Southampton with some interesting shipping in the background.

1963. The VA-2 demonstrating its amphibious capabilities. It was a five-seater craft designed for route evaluation work. It was a fully enclosed craft with retractable sides for easier loading and transportation. It was designed specifically to be transported by air. It had a top speed of 70 mph. It was a big improvement on the VA-1.

This is a view from a helicopter of the VA-2 during operations at Malmö. It was the first demonstration of a British hovercraft in Sweden. Upgraded flexible skirts had been fitted, giving it improved wave riding performance and obstacle clearance.

25 April 1962. The first flight of the VA-3. The new 12-ton craft had a crew of three and could carry twenty-four passengers. It was 16.7 m long and 8.2 m wide and claimed a top speed of 60 mph.

The photograph shows the VA-3 arriving at Rhyl to commence the world's first passenger service between Rhyl and Wallasey. The return journey cost £2. Crossing the Dee estuary by road took around two hours and this service cut that to 30 minutes.

Marshalling the VA-3 as she come ashore at Rhyl in August, 1962. It ran from 20 July until 16 September, 1962. It suffered with reliability problems and also bad weather issues, subsequently operating on only nineteen days. Her end came when bad weather saw her break her moorings, which resulted in severe damage to her structure .The craft was eventually sunk in the Solent.

VT Hovercraft

The VT-1 built by Vosper Thorneycroft, seen here on a trolley at Portchester in 1969. It is powered by hydro propellers with water jets and steered by twin water rudders. This was not fully amphibious, being fitted with small skegs (a sternward extension of the keel) supporting the controllable pitch propellers. It was 95 feet long (29.1 m) with a cruising speed of 40 knots. It could carry 148 passengers and ten cars. Although designed specifically for commercial use, the company also had an eye on military applications.

Following on from the prototype, two other VT-1 craft were built. However, the sad fact is they were unable to sell them and they ended up being scrapped in 1973. On the first craft the stern ramp and door are replaced by an open promenade deck.

Here, two of a kind can be seen at Vosper Thorneycroft's works, Portchester. Two VT-1s can be seen, with the one nearest the camera being the VT-1 002 outside the erection shop, with the fitting out process about to begin.

May, 1970. The VT-1 on her only visit to Southsea. It was designed to nose up on to an inclined slipway. At Ryde her underwater skegs meant she could not cope with the mile-or-so of sand and could not land there. The sad fact was that not being fully amphibious was a major disadvantage.

VT-1M. This was the first craft produced by Vosper Thorneycroft and was described as semi-amphibious – in other words, it could nose up onto a beach of a suitable slope. This was a man-carrying experimental craft used in various trials including with water jet propulsion. It failed to survive beyond the trial stage. This photograph shows it in Portsmouth Harbour in waterjet stage.

In 1972 the decision was made to convert the prototype VT-1 into a fully amphibious craft to be known as VT-2, which proved to be a technical success. Although trials with the Interservice Hovercraft Trials Unit went well, the craft failed to sell and like the VT-1 sadly ended up being scrapped.

Denny Hovercraft

April, 1962. Denny Brothers' immersed sidewall experimental hovercraft D1, which was first tested on the Clyde in 1961, is seen in the photograph in Southampton. The D1 was built by Dennys in collaboration with Hovercraft Developments of Hythe. It was said to be capable of 20 knots. The craft had no amphibious capability and was intended to be used to study the possibilities of sidewall craft on coastal waters. The company flag, sometimes seen on craft, was white with a blue elephant, symbolising the strength and solidity of the company's products. In the background the Cunard liner *Queen Mary* can be seen.

The Denny D2. In 1963 the D2, a sidewall craft weighing 25 tons and seating eighty passengers, operated on the Thames. Denny Hovercraft Ltd were not able to exploit the potential of their design, but this Thames service showed the technical and economic advantages of sidewall hovercraft with low operating costs and high passenger capacity. The craft was 25.5 m long and 5.9 m wide. A sidewall craft has both an air cushion, like a hovercraft, and twin hulls. When the air cushion is off the vessel is supported by the hulls. One advantage over normal hovercraft is that it is more resistant to slipping sideways as a consequence of sea or wind. The Interservice Hovercraft Trials Unit conducted two trials with this craft looking at drag and performance handling. The results were inconclusive.

Britten Norman Hovercraft

The original Britten-Norman Cushioncraft CC-1 hovering. The craft was designed and built in 1959/60. The first flight saw it become the second hovercraft in the world, behind the SRN1. The height of the hover was 12–15 inches (0.30–0.38 m). The photograph shows Mr Britten and Mr Norman.

The CC-1 was built by Cushioncraft, which was a subsidiary of Britten-Norman of Bembridge, Isle of Wight. Between 1960 and 1972 Cushioncraft were to design six models, of which five were produced. In 1972 Cushioncraft was sold to the British Hovercraft Association after Britten-Norman experienced financial problems. The CC1 was difficult to control; it had no skirt and the undercarriage had wheels, supposedly to give better control. The next Cushioncraft model was to be quite different.

A Bristol Belvedere landing a CC1 craft off the Bembridge coast, Isle of Wight. It was to be taken to RAF Chivenor via Lee-on-the-Solent. 1962. The CC1 had been lifted from Bembridge Airport.

The CC-2 was initially designed without a skirt, but over the years had one added in addition to two external engines driving propellers. Originally it carried eleven passengers and two crew. It was 30 feet (9.14 m) long and three were built with military applications in mind. It is therefore no surprise that it was used by the RAF Establishment, Bedford, for research programmes.

The CC-4 was a joint development between Cushioncraft and Hovercraft Development. Subsequent to development use it was sold to Hovercraft Development Ltd/NPL Hovercraft Group, where it was renamed the HU-4. It was used for research into such things as fan propulsion systems.

The CC-7 was developed as a high-speed communications hovercraft, fully amphibious, capable of crossing sand, swamp, ice, etc at speeds up to 50 knots. It was designed with a wide variety of civil and military roles in mind. It could climb gradients up to 1:6 and in waves of 3–4 feet. It could carry eight to ten passengers. It was built in aluminium with inflatable side decks and was the first Cushioncraft to use a gas turbine engine.

Hovercraft in Other Countries

1974. The Voyageur was built by Bell Aerospace, Canada, and was designed to take loads of up to 25 tons over Arctic terrain at speeds of up to 50 mph. By adding superstructure to the flat bed hull, there were many alternative roles – it was tested as a helicopter landing pad. The cargo deck was 40 feet long and 33 feet wide. The caravan was a 'room' for crew use.

1975. Here the 45-ton Voyageur is seen moving through ice on the St Lawrence River. It was capable of breaking through ice 15 inches thick.

A Canadian coastguard Voyageur operating over ice. This was then developed into the LACV-30. The US Navy was so impressed that a huge order was placed.

Voyageur ice-breaking at 15 knots during trials in Montreal on the St Lawrence River in 1975.

US Bell SK5 hovercraft operating in the Plain of Reeds, Vietnam, 1969. The hovercraft carried 1,000 lbs of armour.

Three high-speed LCACs (Landing Craft Air Cushion) Military Assault Hovercraft built for the US Navy by Bell Textron Marine.

A variation. This shows a US Army LACV-30, a lighter amphibian built for the US Army. It has a 30-ton payload. This modular, rugged development of the Voyageur was to be fitted with a bow-mounted swing crane and a bow ramp with logistic support very much in mind.

A US LCAC (Landing Craft Air Cushion) Military Assault Hovercraft showing its capabilities. Basically a stretched Voyageur for the US Army. Twenty-four were built.

An LCAC1 (Landing Craft Air Cushion) Military Assault Hovercraft first production craft, seen entering the well deck of USS *Whidbey Island*, a dock-landing ship of the US Navy.

A Bell Aerospace hovercraft from the early 1960s. It was a test hovercraft for the US military.

1962. *Raduga* (Rainbow), the first hovercraft built by the Krasnoye Sormovo shipyard at Gorky. It was a five-seater, constructed from riveted aluminium sheets. It was 31 feet long, weighed three tons and was powered by two air-cooled piston aircraft engines, reportedly from wartime aircraft. Its top speed was 75 mph and it was designed initially for small rivers where sand bars and shoals made normal navigation impossible.

AIST craft. Very large craft, comparable to the SRN4. Used by the Soviet Navy and heavily armoured. Twenty-four were built using SRN4 lift fans.

The French Naviplane N-300, 1966. Two craft were originally built as open freighters but completed as all-passenger carriers. They could seat ninety passengers without cars, or fifty with six cars. It was built by Sedam and was the first full-scale Naviplane designed for commercial use. During the summer of 1970 the N-300s operated a service along the Cote D'Azur.

Two N-300s photographed in 1969. The N-300 was 24 m in length and 10.5 m wide. The skirt depth was 2 m and the cruising speed was 45–50 knots. Its weight was 27 tons.

1977. The French-built Sedam N-500. Two craft were built to compete with the SRN4s on the cross-channel route from Dover to Calais. They had two decks and one of the obvious differences of the new craft was its skirt, made up of some forty-eight independent skirts, with half around the periphery and the rest forming an inner layer. The skirts were the idea of Bertin, who was an advocate of the multi-skirt approach, using smaller cylindrical skirts instead of one large one. On the outside the very large pressure cells stood out, but to many it was an overcomplicated and unnecessary system. The craft had a seating capacity of 385 and forty-five cars, which was smaller than the original design capacity and meant the capacity was lower than the SRN4 Mk3s. Only two craft were built and they proved a disaster.

Sadly the craft were beset by problems. One was destroyed by fire after only seven running hours. The other craft proved constantly unreliable in spite of expensive modifications and was withdrawn from service in 1983, later to be broken up in 1985. The craft were 50 m long, 23 m wide and when hovering 17 m high. The photograph was taken in 1983.

Early 1960s. Looks familiar? A Mitsubishi-built 3-ton research craft – the Japanese version of our SRN1.

The Armed Forces and Hovercraft

1968. SRN6 hovercraft XV859 operating in Sparrow Cove, a remote bay near Port William on the Falkland Islands. Here was the wreck of SS *Great Britain*. The ship had spent forty-seven years as a floating warehouse but in 1937, becoming too unsafe even for this, she was scuttled in Sparrow Bay. She was, however, rescued and brought back to Bristol in 1970, where she can be seen today. The hovercraft operated in the Falklands from 1967 to 1972.

A Naval Party was commissioned in September 1967 and one hovercraft left the UK in October as deck cargo bound for the Falklands. Its main task was to transport twelve fully equipped Royal Marines to any position in the Falkland Islands day or night. In addition the craft was used for such tasks as aircraft spotting, mail, medical supplies, stores and taking emergency patients from remote areas to hospital. The governor was often taken to visit outlying settlements in the SRN6. The SRN6 is XV859 (027). No hovercraft took part in the Falklands War in 1982.

1968. XV859 (027) in the Falklands. The terrain clearly provided a test for skirt wear and performance. On returning to the UK in 1972 the craft was refurbished and returned to HMS *Daedalus*, where it was used for driver training and general logistic tasks.

1965. SRN5 XT492 in Singapore. This is one of two military versions of the SRN5 modified for operations in the tropics by the Interservice Hovercraft Unit (Far East). Preliminary trials were held in Singapore, lasting for two months. The craft were shipped to and from Singapore as deck cargo. The trials here and elsewhere in the Far East included logistic support of ground forces, naval patrolling, night operations and performance overland and on water.

1966. This time the action is on home soil at Browndown, Gosport, where the SRN5 is used in a support role. The occasion is the Hovershow. The hovercraft is XT492, the same one that was in Singapore the year before. Upon her return the craft was operated by 200 Squadron RCT until 1970 when she was refurbished.

1966. Exercises at Browndown, where a landing craft and the SRN3 dominate the scene.

1966. Two SRN6s followed by two SRN5s.

Hovershow 1966. The SRN5 steals the show again. Trials showed the craft was an effective logistic support craft; a suitable craft for crossing dangerous rapids; an effective and efficient naval patrol craft; and an excellent amphibious craft with superior performance over any conventional amphibian.

This shows an SRN1 Mk1 at Farnborough Airshow in 1959.

An interesting photograph taken in Hong Kong of an RN Patrol Unit. The hovercraft, XV615, is an SRN6 craft that was used in Hong Kong from August 1979. Unfortunately it was damaged while being loaded for shipment back to the UK.

February 1968. SRN6 Mk 2 crossing the sea wall at RAF Chivenor, where it was based for surf trials at Saunton Sands on the North Devon coast.

200 Hovercraft Squadron RCT in exercises in the Far East. Hovercraft of 200 Hovercraft Squadron make a beach landing during Exercise Lath on the east coast of Malaysia. 200 Hovercraft Squadron RCT, based at Browndown, was formed in 1966 and disbanded in 1974. SRN6 Mk2 XV615 can again be identified in the photograph.

SRN5 in Sabah State, North Borneo, with the Interservice Hovercraft Unit (Far East) in 1965 proved to be an effective logistic support craft. Note the long houses in the background. Sabah State was later to merge into what became the Federation of Malaysia.

Above: An SRN6 undergoing trials with the Egyptian Navy. This craft is seen with wire-guided missiles.

Right: 1966. The next two photographs show SRN5 XT657 on exercise in the Solent with HMS *Fearless*. This hovercraft, together with XT493, were converted in 1971/2 to create the SRN6 Mk5 Welldeck craft.

February, 1966. SRN5 XT657 enters the well deck of HMS *Fearless* on what was possibly a press day for the upcoming Hovershow.

Photograph from the early 1960s showing one of the SRN5 craft (destined to be converted into an SRN6 Mk5, or Welldeck) alongside HMS *Bulwark*.

An SRN5 hovercraft negotiating the Pelagus Rapids, Borneo. This was with the Interservice Hovercraft Unit (Far East).

1965. SRN5 hovercraft passing an LCA (Landing Craft Assault) in the river complex around the Tawau area of North Borneo. Trials were being held with two SRN5s by the Interservice Hovercraft Unit (Far East), looking in particular at how effective hovercraft were as a general military load carrier in this type of terrain. The trials showed it was indeed an effective logistic support.

In 1966 trials successfully demonstrated the potential of the SRN5 as a fire fighting and rescue craft. Here XT657 is seen in an exercise.

One of the four SRN5s in service with the Interservice Hovercraft Unit showing her paces at the Hovershow in 1966. It really proved to be a cutting-edge craft.

There was only one SRN3, which is seen here at the Hovershow in 1966 demonstrating her versatility.

Men of the Singapore Guard Regiment brought ashore by an SRN6 Mk2 hovercraft of 200 Hovercraft Squadron RCT. They are simulating an attack on an oil refinery during a demonstration for the Singapore government and armed forces.

An SRN6 Mk2, XV615, on the beach during Exercise Lath, held on the east coast of Malaysia with 200 Hovercraft Squadron RCT around 1971. It subsequently visited Australia.

An SRN6, part of the Egyptian Navy, in mine-laying trials. Note the concrete mock ups.

Above: Three SRN6 hovercraft, having being shipped with one SRN5 craft, arrive at Singapore with 200 Squadron RCT. They would later visit Australia.

Right: Two Welldeck hovercraft, a CC7 and an SRN6 Mk2, in the Solent waiting to be loaded aboard ship en route to Norway for winter trials circa 1972/3. Note the wider bow door on the SRN6 for gun carriage loading. There is also the retractable canvas roof to facilitate loading.

Hover Platforms

The hover barge or platform works like a hovercraft, utilising an air cushion skirt, and is used for moving heavy loads on a cushion of air. They have been developed since the 1970s. This is a Mackace Hoverplatform under tow across Maplin Sands, mudflats off Foulness Island near Southend-on-Sea. Mackace, or Mackley Air Cushion Equipment, produced a number of successful hover barges. Formed in 1971, Mackace offered a solution to the civil engineering problem area of the foreshore, or tidal zone. The idea was to have a craft that could hover over soft ground at low tide, float at high tide and be able to take refuge on any beach if a storm blew up, using an air cushion platform. The company sold hover platforms across the world. In 1979 BHC took over the patents and world trading rights of J.T. Mackley and the new company Mackace Ltd was formed.

Another Mackace hover platform towed by a caterpillar truck. Mackace was based at Funtley near Fareham. Their platforms could be assembled in any part of the world, thus reducing initial costs.

This photograph shows a Mackace Hover barge on the Yukon during trials – shortly before it was badly damaged by fire in December 1974. The roll on, roll off platform was to take personnel and trucks across the 3,500-foot-wide river at Fairbanks, where the Alyasha Pipeline Service were building the Alaska pipeline.

The Mackace Hover barge could carry huge payloads and works like a standard marine barge with an air cushion system that enables it to hover, and when off-hover, as in the photograph, it will still float like a standard marine barge.

This is a Bell Voyageur shown during cold weather trials in Canada. The trials were successful, with one conclusion being very heavy loads could be carried without consuming large amounts of extra fuel.

A Voyageur offloads its cargo of oil drums at Tuktoyatuk in the north-west territories of Canada. Ice-locked ships in the background have to wait out the winter – not so, the Voyageur. It could carry 25 tons at speeds up to 60 mph. Since its payload was equal to that of most transport aircraft it could provide a direct transport link in the remoter regions and a direct link to settlements and operating bases. It was used by the Northern Transport Company.

From the large to the small. Here is a self-propelled Cargo Platform craft from Canada carrying a light cargo.

Unusual, Experimental and Small Hovercraft

The Hover Rover aimed to solve the problem of crop spraying. It was developed to minimise ground pressure and allow the vehicle to cross boggy ground.

The idea of a hovercar appeals to the imagination, but this Hover Rover proved to be a relatively short-lived project. It was not a success and wasn't developed further.

1962. The Terraplane BC4 experimental vehicle was designed by R. Bertin, the same man behind the skirts of the N-500. He developed a series of prototype designs that he called 'naviplanes' if designed for water, and 'terraplanes' if designed for land.

It was completed at the end of 1961 and trials commenced in January, 1962. This was the first flexible petticoat vehicle in the world. On this craft the eight large pads, or rubber fabric bells, each with a diameter of 1.55 m, look very much like elephants' feet.

The Terraplane was a simple design with a platform 7.9 m long and 3.25 m wide that could lift a total weight of 2 tons. Here it is being put through its paces before the press at Satory camp near Paris in 1962.

An air cushion vehicle that is a little different. The ACV-1 was an experimental craft from Ford. Note the brush-like skirt on what is a hover lorry, designed to investigate off-road travel at high speed.

1959. A Cardington hovercraft. Cardington was known for its work on barrage balloons, then airships. It was therefore natural for it to look at inflated structures resistant to damage, easy to repair and of low cost. One of the first was called 'the magic mat'. It was the first inflatable hovercraft made using an air-sea rescue dinghy as a base. The front skids, intended for braking, were ineffective. Its speed over a flat surface was 7 mph and it was powered by a 90cc engine.

Another experimental inflatable hovercraft from the Research Development Establishment at RAF Cardington. Note the mock Scammel truck front. The angle of the photograph suggests it was much bigger than it actually was. The Cardington team pioneered the idea of inflatable hovercraft and fired the imagination! The craft were developed between 1959 and 1961.

Various project craft were produced at the Research Development Establishment at Cardington and their work pioneered the idea of inflatable hovercraft. Those produced included *Bubbles*, *Krafty Kushion*, *Kittykawk*, *Flihi*, *Flilo* and *Krikey*. *Flilo* can be seen here.

An Osprey catamaran concept hovercraft. It looks good but sadly it was a failure.

Saab 401 hovercraft. 'Marinen' is Swedish for 'Navy'. This experimental 40-knot craft was built in 1963 for trials but only one was ever built.

2006. A Griffon hovercraft on a visit to Greenland waters.

The Griffon craft ashore in the testing terrain of Greenland.

A hovercraft designed by the Swiss inventor Karl Wiedland and built in the USA.

Alaska Hovercraft, circa 1983.

Where it All Began

Back to the beginning and the man who deserves the credit for inspiring the development of hovercraft. Here is Sir Christopher Cockerell in July 1959 on the first cross-channel crossing.

It's all over. The craft makes it to Dover in two hours and three minutes!

Hope you enjoyed the photographs. We have now reached the end of the journey… now how do I stop this hovercraft? Let's see what happens when I pull this one.